RICHES TO RAGS
TO RICHES

RICHES TO RAGS TO RICHES

The Power of Tithing

HEIDI GUTTMAN

iUniverse, Inc.
Bloomington

Riches to Rags to Riches
The Power of Tithing

iUniverse books may be ordered through booksellers or by contacting:

iUniverse
1663 Liberty Drive
Bloomington, IN 47403
www.iuniverse.com
1-800-Authors (1-800-288-4677)

ISBN: 978-1-4759-5140-0 (sc)
ISBN: 978-1-4759-5141-7 (hc)
ISBN: 978-1-4759-5142-4 (ebk)

Printed in the United States of America

iUniverse rev. date: 09/24/2012

All Scripture quotes are from The Message Bible unless stated otherwise

ACKNOWLEDGMENTS

I would like to thank Our Father God, Jesus and the Holy Spirit for loving me so much and for never forsaking me when I have wanted to give up on myself so many times. Words cannot express my love and my thankfulness to my Creator!

With heartfelt gratitude I want to thank my wonderful mom and dad for always being there for me and my children. They have been with me through thick and thin and I can always count on them for anything! I have the deepest respect and love for them!

To my three beautiful, loving children Lexi, Cindy and Joshua I give thanks. I want to thank you from the bottom of my heart for loving me so much and standing by me through the good and bad times. I love you all three so much from the depths of my heart, words cannot express. I am so very proud of all three of you, it's amazing. Without you I would be lost. I thank our Father God for you every day.

My deepest love and admiration I have for my older brother Bill and my younger sister Jeanine. Thank you for being the best brother and sister anyone could hope for. You both are truly a blessing to me.

I thank God for graciously placing me in a church that doesn't water down the Word of God and tells it like it is. I am without words at the thankfulness I have for my Senior Pastor and his wife, Pastor Robb Thompson and Linda Thompson. I want to thank them for helping me and my children through some very, difficult, life changing times and I want to thank them for their awesome teaching and genuine love and concern for me and my family.

This book would not have been even possible without a very special and dear friend. I would like to thank my good friend Angie Leszczak from the depths of my heart who always encouraged me to get started on this book. Thank you Angie for editing this book for me. Had it not been for your encouragement I never would have written this book! You are an amazing woman and I am so blessed to know you.

My beautiful friend Joanne I would also like to thank! You are such a talented artist who created the most amazing cover for my book. Words cannot express how beautiful you have made my book!

Finally I would like to thank my former Senior Pastor, Pastor George Thomas who gave me my book title. I told him that I was going to write a book called *From Riches to Rags*. With great excitement I explained to him what the content of my book was going to be. After listening to my explanation he said I should title my book "From Riches to Rags to Riches"! And that is exactly what I did! So thank you Pastor Thomas!

INTRODUCTION

The writing of this book had been on my mind for many, many years. I hadn't put pen to paper (or today fingers to keys) because I struggled with the title. I wanted to title the book from *Riches to Rags*. This was because I had been waiting for years to become rich again like I used to be so I could title this book *From Riches to Rags to Riches* and thought once that happened, I would then write this book. However, I had to correct my thinking about what the word *rich* truly means. How I defined rich was *materialistic riches*. I postponed the writing of this book because I had eagerly waited for my riches to come in the form of money and *stuff*. That's what I knew. That's what I was used to. That's what I *thought* rich was. And oh how wrong I was.

I finally came to the conclusion that I could write this book and title it just as I always wanted to, *From Riches to Rags,* but with an add-on, *to Riches*. Although I am not rich as far as money and materialistic things are concerned, I am rich in my walk with my Father God, Jesus Christ and the Holy Spirit. This is where my riches come from and where they lie.

When I first became a believer the people at the church I was attending at that time, almost never talked about tithing in any depth. I look back now and realize how very strange that was. I was a new believer, going to church and didn't know anything about the tithe. I didn't know how it worked and the saddest part of all, I wasn't being taught the *entire* Word of God. I didn't have a clue about the tithe. This is why I am writing this book to tell you that tithing is *so very important*. It is what GOD *expects of us* and it works! I am living proof that tithing works. This book is my testimony and I pray that you will be open to what I am writing because it is so important not only to the production in our lives, but most importantly to God!

The enemy's greatest goal is to keep us from God's Word. The devil knows the power of the Word of God. Remember he was God's worship leader! The devil will do anything to keep you from knowing the truth. He is very conniving and deceitful. He will keep you from accomplishing that which God wants you to do in your life, no matter what that entails. A very real and personal example is how deceiving and distracting the enemy was even in regards to my decision on the titling of this very book. It is amazing how quickly we can get distracted, concerned and caught up in even the smallest decisions. Thanks to Jesus and the outstanding teaching of my pastor, Pastor Robb on the tithe, I now know the truth and I want everyone to know it as well.

The important thing is I am on track now and I am so glad I know the truth. I will never divert from the written Word of God because of the importance, the *clear* commandment and the requirement of my obedience of the tithe. My purpose for writing this book about tithing is it is a burning passion in my life. I am writing this to my brothers and sisters in the Lord, born again believers. People who love the Lord their God with all their heart, all their might and want to do *everything* God commanded them to do in the bible. As far as I am concerned, if it is in the bible . . . *IT'S THE TRUTH!!* This book is not written as an encouragement to do the right thing, although it can be perceived that way, but I am writing this as a *warning* of what will happen if one decides not to obey God and tithe. It is one thing to read in Malachi 3: 8-12 that you should tithe and you will get blessed. It is quite another story to have someone, who is living *today*, write about the woes and blessings in honoring or not honoring the commandment to tithe.

I am very honored and humbled to be able to write this book about our God, His promises, His blessings and His devotion to us, *if only we will obey.* I hope you too will be obedient to God when He says, "*Test me in this . . .*" and see that our God is exactly that. God.

CHAPTER 1

My financial troubles started many years ago quite honestly because I wasn't tithing. I could try making up excuses, but it is what it is. I was not tithing. At that time I was a believer but didn't know anything about the tithe because I hadn't been taught about the tithe. The church I was attending at that time, did not teach about the tithe in depth. Although my money wasn't going into God's house, (I didn't know I was robbing God by not tithing) my money was going into many other people's houses because I would spend my money on other people. At that time in my life I was living it up. I had the ability to buy *anything* my little heart desired because money was never an issue and I had a lot of it! I will be going into great detail about my spending habits and by no means am I boasting. At this point in my life I am not proud of my actions that took place back then. I was spending and spending, for me, for them, for us and I was not giving God one red penny as far as the tithe was concerned. Nada, nothing, zip. Thus the cause of my financial demise.

I had everything a woman could want materialistically. I had a big beautiful townhouse, awesome cars, expensive artwork, many gorgeous furs, a lot of beautiful diamonds and jewelry galore, an awesome Harley, a big beautiful sports yacht and many other extravagant materialistic possessions. Let me emphasize here the word *possessions*. That's something I want you to remember. The word *possessions*.

I would go on shopping sprees *all the time*. I didn't just go shopping because I needed to. I went shopping because *I could*. I wasn't even concerned with what was on sale. Who needed a sale? Who needed a budget? I didn't *need* to save anything! Everything was at my fingertips. My shopping sprees were a habit. Shop 'til ya drop because the money wasn't running out anytime soon. Or so I thought. Although I was spending my money, my money had control of me. And here we *see* the *possess*-ions. Money dictated my life in every way. And definitely not the way God intended, for us to dictate money. God first, *then* shall all these things be added unto you. In Matthew 6:33 the NIV version says, "But seek first his kingdom and his righteousness, and all these things will be given to you as well. Therefore do not worry about tomorrow, for tomorrow will worry about itself. Each day has enough trouble of its own."

The problem I was encountering was I was trying to fill a void in my life. Although I am not sure I knew it at the time, my Spirit did. This void's name was loneliness. I squelched my loneliness by *shopping*. It worked for a very short time. A sort of anesthetic. The next time I felt lonely, here came my fix. Some shopping mall or store yelling for me to come and shop, shop, shop. Come and find relief. Get your quick fix here. However, the relief was not to come from *possess*-ions, but it was to come from my Creator, God Almighty, the one who gave it all up for me, Jesus Christ.

When I was going through this my three kids were all small. What a perfect reason to go shopping! "It's for the children!" Oh brother. But unfortunately when my flesh screamed and my fingers found my wallet, off I went. I would go into the high end stores children's department. I would spend $800 in the girl's department on my two daughters. And of course that wouldn't be enough because now my son needed new stuff too. I wouldn't have wanted him to have felt unloved. So naturally, the only fair thing to do was to go to the boy's department and spend $500 in just a few short minutes. My kids were only allowed to wear designer clothes, such as Tommy Hilfiger, The Gap, and Gymboree, just to name a few, but you get the picture. Only name brands graced the closets of my children. Nothing was too expensive for them, because money was in abundance!

However, I was placing myself as God in their life. I was meeting their every need. They didn't *need* God. Mom provided! If I had continued on that path, my children would not be trusting God *for anything* today. Not only did I rob God of my tithe, but I would have also robbed Him of the devotion, trust, admiration and love from my children that God so deserves and most of all the joy God gets from providing for my children. I would have once again robbed God not only in *one* area of my life, but all areas of my *children's* lives as well.

One of my most very embarrassing moments, came during one of the spending frenzies. My husband and I had a high chair made out of white leather. Can you even imagine leather for a baby? Talk about wasteful and extravagant! And if that wasn't enough, almost on a regular basis I would take my kids into the toy store FAO Schwartz and buy them *whatever they wanted*. In Romans 12:1-2 the bible says, "So here's what I want you to do, God helping you: Take your everyday, ordinary life—your sleeping, eating, going-to-work, and walking-around life—and place it before God as an offering. Embracing what God does for you is the best thing you can do for him. Don't become so well-adjusted to your culture that you fit into it without even thinking. Instead, fix your attention on God. You'll be changed from the inside out. Readily recognize what he wants from you, and quickly respond to it. Unlike the culture around you, always dragging you down to its level of immaturity, God brings the best out of you, develops well-formed maturity in you." I was my kids dream come true! I was my children's very own fairy godmother! Sadly to say, God wasn't anywhere to be found in my generosity.

I think back and am so ashamed of the fool-heartedly waste I succumbed to. Not only did I trudge willingly through the world's way, I dragged my children with me. I remember buying my oldest girl a huge bear for hundreds of dollars. It was never a problem. I used to take them to the American Girl Doll Place on Michigan Avenue like clockwork and buy them the latest doll, doll clothes and accessories. I even took the dolls to their hair stylist to get the latest hairdo. We would have tea in the tearoom every time we went! And for you moms who know of this store and the price tags that go along with this, you can see the *out of control* behavior I was exhibiting. Over the top doesn't even start to describe my behavior.

But the kids weren't the only ones to get spoiled. My husband and I would go to many art shows and buy whatever we liked without ever thinking about the cost. A painting for $1000? No problem. Buy it! A beautiful, acrylic, geometric sculpture for $8000? Mine! Buy it! Nothing was out of my reach. We would go out to eat at expensive restaurants *with our kids* all the time.

We would live on our boat every weekend. Our home away from home. And here is the saddest part. We even skipped church on Sunday's because we were on our boat. Although I loved God, stuff was my life. I think of the amount of money we spent just on gas and I so wish I would have given that to God! We would spend around $800.00 just on gas for the boat for the weekend! This was not including dining out or shore excursions. Life was good. But, I keep asking myself, where was God in this picture? He wasn't.

CHAPTER 2

What you need to understand is that I loved God. I loved the Lord so much. I remember as a child going to my maternal, German grandmother's house in Hannover, Germany on special occasions such as the holidays to visit her. She was such a caring and loving person filled with so much grace and elegance. Oh how I loved her and how I looked up to her. She loved God and Jesus with all of her heart, soul and mind. She led me to the Lord when I was young, praise God! She always talked to me about God and the Bible. I remember asking her questions about God while I was visiting her. She would always say in the German language "we have a great and glorious God" (my mom and her brother said that a lot). When she would tuck me in at night at her apartment, she would tell me to repeat after her when she prayed and I did. She taught me how to pray in German. I continued to pray in the German language for many years. Praying in the German language always made me feel close to God (since that was the first language I ever communicated to God in). When I started praying in the English language it was kind of strange for me at first because I wasn't used to praying in English. Praying in German came so natural and easy to me. I could feel God's presence while I prayed.

My grandmother would always talk about my grandfather, who passed away before I was born, with so much love. I thank God for placing my grandmother into my life when He did. She was such a blessing! My granddad died in the war. During WWII my grandfather was in the city of Bordeaux which is in France. He spoke six languages and because he was multi-lingual he was forced to be an interpreter at the courts which were dealing with war crimes. This bothered him a great deal, since he was a Christian. Grandfather was later sent home to Hannover, Germany because the Nazis were letting some of the older soldiers, go home. He was then teaching at the middle school in Hannover. He was supposed to be the principal there, but because of his faith, as a Christian, he did not get the job. He then became an air raid warden in his neighborhood. His job was to walk down the streets and check on his neighbors to make sure that they were safe. At night, during the bombings, he would walk down the streets and make sure all of the lights were turned off, as to not attract any of the enemy airplanes that were flying around waiting to attack.

God is with us in good and bad times. This was true for my grandfather as well. And we also need to remember that bad things happen to good people. This too applied to my grandfather. The evening of October 8th 1943, 23 of my grandfather's neighbors were hiding in his shelter while the enemy was attacking by air. The shelter got hit by a bomb, damaging the door of the shelter. The people wanted out of the shelter but they couldn't escape because the wooden door was damaged and jammed. My grandfather was in the street when news reached him of what had happened to the shelter at his house. He went back to his house with a hand saw and started to saw the door in order to rescue all of the people. While he was sawing the door, another bomb came, hit the shelter and all of the 23 people died including my grandfather.

After this atrocity happened, the remaining German people in my grandfather's city did not do anything to try to find the bodies, since they were buried under rubble. My Grandmother's brother was a mayor in one of the neighboring towns and he sent in a special crew to my grandparent's house to try to find my grandfather's body. After three weeks of digging, they finally found his body. When they dug my grandfather out, he was still holding the square saw in both his hands. On September 29th 1943, my mom, her brother, two sisters and my grandmother were evacuated from their home. Nine days later the Americans bombed the town again, including my grandfather's house. Had they stayed around they would have been killed. God is so good. He was protecting the remaining family members. My family was evacuated to a small town where they stayed with another relative, they were allowed to stay in a very small room. You have to know that my mother's family was very wealthy before the war. They lived in a big house. And even though they had to share a small room, during this terrible time, they felt so blessed and thankful to God that their lives had been spared!

In 1957, before she met my dad, my mother went to Madrid, Spain to study linguistics. She was 23 years old. (Today she speaks five languages fluently. I have to brag a little! She takes after her dad.) My dad was in the American Air Force at the time, stationed at Torreon Air Force Base. My dad met my mom and they fell in love. He asked my mom to marry him and she said yes. As every young girl desires, she wanted her mother's blessing. However, when she told her mother, my grandmother became very upset and told my mom she would never bless the marriage of her daughter to an American because the American's killed her dad. But my mom was very persistent and would not give up, seeking the blessing from her mother. My mom told my grandmother that my dad was a good man, a man to be admired and that he would take good care of her. She told her mother it was not my dad's fault her husband had been killed by an American. What was the sense of my dad having to pay for the bombing that killed my grandfather? So as you may have already guessed my grandmother finally gave my mother her blessing to go ahead and marry my dad. Later, I was born in Madrid on the Torreon Air Force Base.

However, even with all of that history poured into me, and the love my grandmother showed me, as well as the stories she shared of how in love her and my grandfather were, there was nothing portraying God in my life outside of church. I didn't know the God my grandmother knew. I went to church as much as I could, when I could. When it was convenient. In the summer I did not attend on Sunday's because spending time on our boat was our family time. I remember hearing our wonderful senior pastor, Pastor Robb preach one time after boating season was over, on the topic of, *When things are good and you are in abundance don't forget the ONE who provided for you.* That made me think of what I was doing way back then. I had forgotten the giver of all good things. In Ephesians 5:20 the NIV says, ". . . always giving thanks to God the Father for everything, one who provided me the good things.

I don't think I realized what I was doing at the time. That is one of the most detrimental effects of *stuff*. It gets to be so big in your life you start to think *that's just how it is.* Now granted I was on the rich side of life, but this also occurs with those who don't have so much *stuff.* Their *stuff* is not materialistic in manner, but bad thoughts, bad situations, bad relationships and whatever else life at that level throws at you. But, the harm is no different. In either scenario, God is nowhere to be found because the *stuff* is too much. When my kids were very young I bought them a book with the title about, *Too Much Stuff.* I can't remember the exact title of the book which I used to read to all three of them all the time, but I clearly remember the message. The book was about how having too much "materialistic stuff" didn't necessarily mean it would make a person happy. It talked about how having God in your life would make a person happy instead of all the stuff and how we are not going to take any of that stuff with us to heaven. All three of my kids understood that, but yet I was not living that simple truth out in my life that "The blessing of the LORD makes a person rich, and he adds no sorrow with it." (Proverbs 10:22 NLT)

You might be thinking this was the beginning of my turnaround. Nope. I was still spending the money on "stuff". So although I was trying to teach my children the right way, I was not living the right way before them. It was not only evident to me, but it was very evident to my children because no matter what they asked for I would buy it for them. Honestly I cannot ever remember saying no to them, for anything. And now today it is the opposite! I say no a lot. If I don't think they *need* it or if I think it is a waste of money I say "no"! Or I tell them to buy it themselves since both of my girls work. And although my story is sad, I am so happy I have lived through this whole experience because it has strengthened me in the Lord. I now realize stuff does not make me happy. I also know I will not be taking any of it with me to heaven, so, I can take it or leave it. I choose to leave it.

CHAPTER 3

As one might guess, my spending had become an addiction. An idol. Counters at department stores had become my altars to the god of money. It was beyond out of control for me. It was like an addiction. I couldn't stop. Even if I wanted to tame myself, it wasn't going to happen in the natural. I got a rush from it. It made me feel in control of my life. It made me feel important. It made me feel worthy. It made me feel things that I was looking for in relationships. I was trying to fill a void. The emptiness that I felt on the inside through my marriage and because of my abandonment issues was just too much for me. Stuff had become my God. Stuff was my security. Instead of looking to Jesus, who is the Author and Finisher of my faith, I was looking to stuff. It says in Hebrews 12:2 in the NIV, "Let us fix our eyes on Jesus, the author and perfecter of our faith, who for the joy set before him endured the cross, scorning its shame, and sat down at the right hand of the throne of God . . .". I was looking at manna. In today's language we call it material possessions. But I loved Jesus. I just needed to have my focus redirected. The life I was living was selfish. The life I was living looked more like the world instead of God's kingdom. I had become a spoiled brat. A rich, stuck up lady who was only interested in stuff. The more the better! The price you say? Who cares? Bring on the stuff! But, don't get me wrong. I was a nice person. We all are, way deep down inside. Or at least that's one of our reasonings for some of our bizarre behavior. With me it was spending and if I did it for others, well, it just might be okay with God. What I loved about spending money on other people was to experience the joy that people got when they received a gift. That was a rush for me.

You can only imagine what Christmas was like. All the other days of the week seemed like Christmas, but Christmas was different. I had a *reason* to spend. I wanted to bless others. (But still, no gift for God as far as the tithe was concerned.) Christmas was amazing for my whole family, (and beyond) because I spent money so extravagantly. Who needed Santa Claus when they had Heidi? My husband could barely keep up with the bills. That's how quickly I spent money! It wasn't just our three kids that I splurged on. Oh no! The motto of the world is "Share the wealth"! And I did it very well. Not only was it my family, it was also my husband's other four kids and their families. I would buy for mom, dad, brother, sister, aunts, uncles, cousins, my in-laws, you name it! And the want was never too big. One year I helped my sister buy new furniture.

Even before these Christmas' my husband and my spending was so extravagant that we decided to get married in Germany. Just because we could and because, for a rational reason, my parents lived there. Instead of flying my parents to the United States we flew to Germany. Because I had the money, it was mine and it was okay that my husband spent the money for this joyous occasion! My husband flew his whole family from Chicago to Germany for the wedding. I bought my wedding dress on Oak Street in downtown Chicago. The dress cost $12,000.00 but my husband talked them down and got it for less. Now you have to understand Oak Street, in Chicago is the street that millionaires shop on. All of the stores on this street are very high end and are *very* expensive. The average Joe doesn't shop on Oak Street. Hey! A girl gets married only once. Or so they are supposed to. My wedding dress was one of a kind. It was designed after the movie *My Fair Lady*. It was completely beaded and it was beautiful! I had the bridesmaid's dresses custom made in my favorite color, purple. The color of royalty. No expense was held back.

In my world life was good and who was I to question this lucky break in life I had caught? This life consumed me on every level. It just never stopped and to be quite honest, I didn't want it to. I remember my husband taking me to downtown Chicago to New York Jeweler's many times and buying me whatever my heart desired! For you who don't know New York Jeweler's it is a very upscale jewelry store located downtown where prominent people shop. (I met Mayor Daley there once!) Yes, life was good! One year I came home from running errands and my husband had bought me a Harley motorcycle in my favorite colors, purple and black! I had never expressed I wanted a Harley, but there it was. More stuff! I was so excited and thankful. However when I got on it, it was too big for me. It almost tipped over on me! I couldn't even squeeze the clutch. I wasn't strong enough! We had to sell it because I couldn't ride it. It was just too big and too heavy.

Still yet another event to support our spending addiction was, one year I remember going to my jewelry box to put on my engagement ring and wedding band, after cleaning all day, and

I picked up my engagement ring and instead of my one carat diamond, there was a much bigger and perfect diamond which my husband had replaced! Yep, life was good and how I loved God. Or so I thought, in both instances. And how very, very wrong I was, in both instances. Not only was stuff my god, I had also displaced God in my life. I was robbing Him too! In the bible Malachi 3:6-12 says, "I am God—yes, I Am. I haven't changed. And because I haven't changed, you, the descendants of Jacob, haven't been destroyed. You have a long history of ignoring my commands. You haven't done a thing I've told you. Return to me so I can return to you," says God-of-the-Angel-Armies. "You ask, 'But how do we return?' "Begin by being honest. Do honest people rob God? But you rob me day after day. "You ask, 'How have we robbed you?' "The tithe and the offering—that's how! And now you're under a curse—the whole lot of you—because you're robbing me. Bring your full tithe to the Temple. Test me in this and see if I don't open up heaven itself to you and pour out blessings beyond your wildest dreams. For my part, I will defend you against marauders, protect your wheat fields and vegetable gardens against plunderers." The Message of God-of-the-Angel-Armies. "You'll be voted 'Happiest Nation.' You'll experience what it's like to be a country of grace." God-of-the-Angel-Armies says so. This was me.

In Leviticus 27:30-33 the Bible says, "A tenth of the land's produce, whether grain from the ground of fruit from the trees, is God's. It is holy to God. If a man buys back any of the tenth he has given, he must add twenty percent to it. A tenth of the entire herd and flock, every tenth animal that passes under the shepherd's rod, is holy to God. He is not permitted to pick out the good from the bad or make a substitution. If he dishonestly makes a substitution, both animals, the original and the substitute, become the possession of the Sanctuary and cannot be redeemed." This scripture means before we as humans buy any materialistic item, we *need* to give the tithe to God first—before anything!! The tithe is holy to God. Although I loved God, I wasn't obeying His Word.

We must always remember that *everything* God gives us belongs to Him in the first place and He is watching us to see how much we will give back to Him! In the bible 10% is a commandment. It is not whatever *you want to do*! The bible is very clear about this and tells us what to do. In Deuteronomy 14:22-26 the Bible says, "Make an offering of ten percent, a tithe, of all the produce which grows in your fields year after year. Bring this into the Presence of God, your God, at the place he designates for worship and there eat the tithe from your grain, wine, and oil and the firstborn from your herds and flocks. In this way you will learn to live in deep reverence before God, your God, as long as you live. But if the place God, your God, designates for worship is too far away and you can't carry your tithe that far, God, your God, will still bless you: exchange your tithe for money and take the money to the place God, your God, has chosen to be worshiped. Use the money to buy anything you want: cattle, sheep, wine, or beer—anything that looks good to you. You and your family can then feast in the Presence of God, your God, and have a good time."

In Matthew 7:7-12 the Bible says, "Don't bargain with God. Be direct. Ask for what you need. This isn't a cat-and-mouse, hide-and-seek game we're in. If your child asks for bread, do you trick him with sawdust? If he asks for fish, do you scare him with a live snake on his plate? As bad as you are, you wouldn't think of such a thing. You're at least decent to your own children. So don't you think God who conceived you in love will be even better?" If we as sinners want to give good gifts to our children what about our Father in heaven? Don't you think HE wants to give us good gifts? Then the flip side is if we love our Father in heaven, wouldn't we want to give HIM good gifts and be pleasing to Him? That's how the natural relationship between parents and children works. So all the more it should be with us and our heavenly Father. Here is a simple, rule-of-thumb guide for behavior: Ask yourself what you want people to do for you, then grab the initiative and do it for them. Add up God's Law and Prophets and this is what you get."

This scripture makes me think about my three kids. Because I am their mom, I want to provide for them in any way that I can because I love them so much. Not only do I want to provide materialistic things for them that they need and may want, but I also want to provide lots of love, guidance, comfort, support, nurturing, discipline and many other things for them, just as our Father God wants to do for each and every one of us!

CHAPTER 4

Why did God create us? I think about this every day or on a daily basis. The answer is quite simple if we would just read what our bibles say. We were created to be pleasing to *Him*. How can we be pleasing to our heavenly Father who gives us all things as it states in Matthew 7:11, when we steal from Him by not tithing? This is biblical. Remember what Malachi 3:6-12 said? It was *God* who said we were robbing Him. It states that when God told the people they needed to return to Him, this opened up a whole can of worms. They asked the question and God answered it. Just like me. I finally realized after all of that time that I *needed* to tithe in order to be pleasing and obedient to God.

God didn't dance around the question worrying if He was going to offend them or what the repercussions were going to be if He told them that they were thieves. In Numbers 23: 19-21 the Bible says, "God is not man, one given to lies, and not a son of man changing his mind. Does he speak and not do what he says? Does he promise and not come through? I was brought here to bless; and now he's blessed—how can I change that? He has no bone to pick with Jacob, he sees nothing wrong with Israel. God is with them, and they're with him, shouting praises to their King." You need to be careful what you ask God. God is going to answer your question *in* full and when He does you won't have to wonder what He was *really* saying. He told the people that they were *robbing* Him. They asked. He answered.

I don't know about you. But when I get to heaven I will have enough things to answer for and I *do not* want *stealing from* God to be on that list. If you had to answer God about not tithing, what would you say? *He sees everything! He knows everything!* Even into our hearts for our motives! In 1 Corinthians 4:5 the NIV says, "Therefore judge nothing before the appointed time; wait till the Lord comes. He will bring to light what is hidden in darkness and will expose the motives of men's hearts. At that time each will receive his praise from God." Think about this. As children did we steal from our parents? Most people would respond by saying "no", right? Stealing from our parents for most people was and is unthinkable and unacceptable. It does not matter how good or bad our relationship was with them. It doesn't matter what the need, how big or small the need was. You don't steal from your parents! If we don't steal from our parents why would we ever consider stealing from God? We should fear God more than we fear our parents!

I remember a day when I was feeling like the world was good—things were looking up, I was at church, the senior pastor, Pastor Robb got my attention as he always does. He made an announcement one Sunday morning and it truly broke my heart. He said, "Make sure you keep an eye on your purses, ladies, because people in this room steal from God so they would not hold back from stealing from you." How heart-breaking that was to me and so true! People can and do steal from God! After hearing that from my pastor I now watch my purse very closely during service, which I never did before. How sad.

To me tithing encompasses so much more than money. It is commitment, faithfulness, love, gratefulness, surrender and intimacy with Our Father God. I want to be pleasing to God and I want HIM to be proud of me. Therefore I tithe. In the book of Nehemiah the author talks about the tithe quite often which means the tithe is very important! Let's look at some of these passages from Nehemiah and meditate on them.

In Nehemiah 10:38 the Bible says, "We'll see to it that a priest descended from Aaron will supervise the Levites as they collect the tithes and make sure that they take a tenth of the tithes to the treasury in the Temple of our God." This passage tells us that God has established the action of tithing to be important because HE assigns a priest descended from Aaron to oversee the tithe. In Nehemiah 12:44 the Bible says, "That same day men were appointed to be responsible for the storerooms for the offerings, the first fruits, and the tithes. They saw to it that the portion directed by the Revelation for the priests and Levites was brought in from the farms connected to the towns. Judah was so appreciative of the priests and Levites and their service; they, along with the singers and security guards, had done everything so well, conducted the worship of their God and the ritual of ceremonial cleansing in a way that would have made David and his son Solomon proud. That's the way it was done in the olden days, the days of David and Asaph, when they had choir directors for singing songs of praise and thanksgiving to God." In this passage God talks about how King David and King Solomon, the two most awesome kings ever in history, would have been honored to tithe because they wanted to show God how much they respect God and who He is. This means the tithe is to be celebrated and respected, since we respect God and celebrate God we should respect and celebrate tithing.

Remember when Kind David brought the Ark of the Covenant into the city of David and he was celebrating and dancing as he was entering the city? He didn't care who was watching him nor what people thought of him because he was so *in love* with God. I think we should celebrate the tithe this way. We should tithe with great enthusiasm, with dancing and praise to God! Look at it for yourselves. In 2 Samuel 6:12-16 it says, "It was reported to King David that God had prospered Obed-Edom and his entire household because of the Chest of God. So David thought, I'll get that blessing for myself," and went and brought up the Chest of God from the house of Obed-Edom to the city of David, ceremonially dressed in priest's linen, danced with great abandon before God. The whole country was with him as he accompanied the Chest of God with shouts and trumpet blasts. But as the chest of God came into the city of David, Michal, Saul's daughter, happened to be looking out a window. When she saw King David leaping and dancing before God, her heart filled with scorn." Saints, let me ask you a question. Are you hung up on which person is watching you (maybe in church) during worship or are you more interested in *entering in* while you are worshiping our Lord? It's a question that all of us need to ponder on. Remember everything we do we do unto the Lord, not unto man and that includes tithing.

Nehemiah 13:4 in the NIV says, "Before this, Eliashib the priest had been put in charge of the storerooms of the house of our God. He was closely associated with Tobiah, and he had provided him with a large room formerly used to store the grain offerings and incense and temple articles, and also the tithes of grain, new wine and oil prescribed for the Levites, singers and gatekeepers, as well as the contributions for the priests." This passage shows the importance of storing the tithes and offerings. Saints, why do you think this is so important? It has to do with obedience. The Lord wants to see if we will be obedient to Him.

A few verses down in verses 12 and 13 it says, "I got everyone back again and put them back on their jobs so that all Judah was again bringing in the tithe of grain, wine and oil to the storerooms. I put Shelemiah the priest, Zadok the scribe, and a Levite named Pedaiah in charge of the storerooms. I made Hanan son of Zaccur, the son of Mattaniah, their right-hand man. These men had a reputation for honesty and hard work. They were responsible for distributing the rations to their brothers." Here God reveals how important it is to have men who are honest, who can be trusted to protect the tithe and to distribute it accordingly. If the tithe was not important to Our Father God, He wouldn't be appointing priests to oversee and take care of "the tithe". If the tithe was not important to Our Father God anyone could take care of it, right? That is why it is so important for us to bring our tithes to our local church, a place that we as believers can trust, since we love God and His house.

It saddens me when I know people are stealing from God, without even giving it a second thought. We are to honor our God. How can we possibly honor God when we are withholding the tithe? It is rightfully His to begin with, isn't it? When we withhold our tithes, we are robbers! We should willingly want to give to God because we love Him. Remember when I told you in the introduction that there is only one time in the entire bible that God *instructs* us to test Him? In Malachi 3:10 God tells us, almost to the point of demanding us to test Him in giving Him the tithe. And if that's not enough He continues with the blessing that will occur *if* and when we do this. He tells us to tithe *and then* He will open the windows of heaven and pour out His blessings on us. How awesome is that? God instructs us to do something He has commanded, which is to be obedient, and because of His love for us, will bless us for being obedient! Just as we who are parents bless our children for being obedient.

A question that often haunts my thoughts as a believer is if a person *truly* is a believer, why wouldn't that person want to test God? Again Malachi 3:10 the Bible says, "Bring your full tithe to the Temple treasury so there will be ample provisions in my Temple. Test me in this and see if I don't open up heaven itself to you and pour out blessings beyond your wildest dreams." What does a person who doesn't tithe have to lose if he decides to tithe? And if we can't trust God to keep His Word in this context, why do we believe we are saved and going to heaven? Do we truly believe the Word when it says in Numbers 23:19-20 of the NIV, "God is not a man, that he should lie, nor a son of man, that he should change his mind. Does he speak and then not act? Does he promise and not fulfill? I have received a command to bless; He has blessed, and I cannot change it."

It is quite simple. Either the bible is all true or it's not. Someone recently said to me, "I can't afford to tithe." What a misconception this is! This person is missing the whole point of tithing! If a person tithes than he/she will have plenty to live off of. But if that person chooses *not* to tithe, than he/she will always live in lack and want. The tithe belongs to Him, right? The bible is a black, white and red document. Literally. Either we believe *all* of it, or we believe none of it.

If we give God the 10% (the tithe) He requests of us, then He will be faithful and give us more. Here is where the testing ties in again. We need to look at the tithe as something that does not belong to us in the first place; therefore as soon as we get paid 10% should go straight to our local church with *no* questions whatsoever. We would never think of requesting from our employer that they cease taking taxes out of our checks, because we can't afford to have that amount withheld. And here is something to think about. The IRS takes an *average* of 20% of our checks for taxes! And God only asks for 10%, willingly. It is sad how so many people do not even want to talk about tithing. These type of people act as if it's not spoken about, it does not exist. That is crazy thinking! We don't talk about our air intake, but air exists!

CHAPTER 5

God has done so many miracles and wonders in my life it brings me to tears. I have been tithing for over 10 years now, every single time I get a paycheck, without missing a beat. It has been an amazing journey. I am going to share some of these with you. There came a day, years ago, when I could no longer afford my house as a single parent. I had fallen behind in my mortgage payments and things started snowballing in a heavily negative way. I put my house on the market (which is my dream home that I built) and tried so hard so many times to sell it (even one of my former pastors and his wife came by to look at my house to see if they wanted to buy it). But, much to my dismay it would not sell! And definitely unbeknownst to me, God had other plans for me! Thanks to God I still reside in this house today!

Not only were bill collectors threatening me, it seemed like everybody simultaneously had collaborated together to destroy me; the constant pummeling of my psyche with the never ending barraging of threats to take something away from me. I was so desperate I started looking into section 8 (rental housing assistance for low-income households) which I knew nothing about. Now I had begun allowing fear to enter into the equation. I was so scared because all I constantly thought about was the welfare of my three children. There is an important point I want to make here. I had been faithfully tithing *for years* when this happened. One New Year's Eve I was at church when a visiting Pastor prophesied over me. This was the first time I had ever been prophesied over. I want to share an entry I made in my journal:

"After the Pastor was done preaching his message he started prophesying over people. At one point he had people coming to the altar so that he could prophecy over them. I had never had a prophecy before so I was really praying hard for it, when finally the pastor came over to me and he took me by the hand and made me stand up. This is what he said to me, "God says it is not over 'til I say it is over, it's not over 'til I say it's over. Daughter it's not over yet so quit crying, and God said I'm still working on your behalf, it's not time, it's not over, just a short time, a period of six months and you shall see the glory of the Lord. You say what God can do, and God says I can do everything but it's not time yet, and God says when it's over you are going to say Lord I thank you, stay calm, stay put and see the Glory of the Lord."

God is so good that even as an author, I have no words to express my gratefulness to Him. I received my miracle exactly *six months* to the day! On that day I got a phone call from my mom and dad telling me they were going to bail me out with the house since I could not sell it and it had already been on the market twice. They informed me they had decided to take over the house payments for me! They continued to explain to me that they had talked it over with my brother and that he said it would be a great investment for them. I started crying and praising the Lord! It was so hard to contain myself! After I got off the phone with them I thanked and praised the Lord again. What an awesome miracle! You can just imagine my emotional high as just a few weeks prior to this I was looking into section 8 housing and preparing myself psychologically that there was a possibility that me and my children may end up on the street. That was my journal entry!

Although I would love to say it was some mysterious, magical miracle that occurred, that would be absolutely untrue. I knew *exactly* why this had happened. Not only because God loved me and takes care of His children, but I had a promise written in gold. I had received this miracle because of the fact that I was tithing. I had taken God at His Word, tested Him and guess what happened? God made other plans for me! Plans that are not of this world, not of the natural realm, but God had His own, heavenly plans. God breathed plans of the supernatural! We serve a supernatural God; therefore that's how HE works.

As a responsible grown woman, raising three children as a single parent, I was dealing with my situation, but I knew in my heart that God was going to take care of me and my children. To this day I constantly watch the DVD of the prophecy spoken over me. I watch it over and over again reminding myself (and the devil) that my Father, my Provider, my Comforter, my Lord and my King will always come through! He has to. He told me to test Him and I did and I will. I expect nothing less from my awesome God! I waited and waited for six months for the day when I would get my miracle. I never lost faith. I never lost hope. Why? Because I *knew* my Father God would come through. I knew that He was not a man that He should lie and I knew that He wasn't the Son of Man to change His mind. The Word of God said it and I believed it! I had total confidence and great peace that my faithful, awesome, loving Father God would take care of me because He loves me and because I love Him enough that I am obedient to His one command that says, "Test me in this." Therefore I tithed and He fulfilled His promise. I believe had I not been a tither, this miracle would never have happened.

Because I am a human, through this whole process I was trying to figure out how the prophecy was going to happen. What day would it happen? How was God going to bring this to pass? It was so exciting to wait in anticipation to see what the Lord was going to do. However, also during this time the Lord was testing my patience, which as I now realize was good for me. What a great learning experience for me. I constantly had to remind myself what the bible said. Isaiah 55:8-9 in the NIV says, "For my thoughts are not your thoughts, neither are your ways my ways," declares the Lord. "As the heavens are higher than the earth, so are my ways higher than your ways and my thoughts than your thoughts." Therefore I waited. I waited with much anticipation.

After this miracle I wanted to shout the goodness and faithfulness of God from the rooftops! I wanted to tell everyone who would listen to me that God loved me! I wanted everyone to know that God is who He says He is! He *will* do what He says He will! And that the Word of God was true! But, I only found a few who wanted to know the greatness of God and the faithfulness He had demonstrated in my life, not because of the favor I found, but because of obedience to His written word. I even tried to tell some of my family members who were not saved about my miracle, hoping they would realize that God is the author and finisher of our lives, that He is the same provider for us as He was and still is for Israel. But that was not to be. They did not understand or accept what I was telling them. But I did not allow their unbelief to drag me down, burst my bubble or more disastrously yet, allow myself to begin to question and even doubt what God had done for me. I would not allow my humanity, my thoughts, and my always deceiving feelings to waive and start to question my blessing, because I knew my God. I knew what He was capable of. I knew He loved me. I knew He was never late. Above all else, I was so thankful to our Lord and so blown away and in speechless *awe* of Him that nothing could keep me quiet!

I'll never forget the day when I received that news from my parents as long as I live. It was a hot summer day and I was in my backyard tanning and reading God's Word when I got the phone call from my parents. They told me that they talked it over with my brother and they decided it would be a good investment to take over the house payments for me. I love tanning, while reading my bible in the sun. It was (and still is) my favorite past time. I love God's Word. I can never get enough of God's wisdom, instruction, knowledge and insight. I try to study God's Word at least one hour a day (that is my goal and my desire). However, because of life and all of its demands, I have not been able to attain that which I desire. Unfortunately as humans we have responsibilities which include crazy work schedules that consumes many of our waking hours, thus prohibiting our desire to just sit with God, listen for His voice and feed on His word. When I am unable to feed on God's word it literally pains me, as it should for all of us who don't feed on God's Word. Sometimes I am not able to get my full, desired one hour. I look for every opportunity to get into the Word of God. I get a half hour break at work so by the time I arrive at my lunch destination that only leaves me with a few minutes to read my Bible. What this means is that I have to get creative. Is going to lunch more important to me than bringing my lunch to work and just eating in my car? Whatever the solution I pursue will enable me to get back on track again. I have even gone so far as to find a new job! I figure once I get my new job I will be able to take an hour lunch, the time I so badly need and want to read God's Word.

The Word of God is like a hidden treasure chest. You have the map with the X on it, but in order to get to the X, you need to constantly be studying the map. That is why I love when I have a day off of work and have the ability to sit in peace and read my Bible as long as I want to. It is such a good feeling to me, so comforting, so peaceful, so helpful, and so REWARDING. Want to hear something cool, since writing the above paragraph I have recently started a new job which is what I have been praying for! God is so great I now have the time during my day at work to read the Word of God for one hour! Praise God!

I began to pour myself into earnestly reading the bible back in 2001. Since then I have read the bible completely through from the Old Testament to the New Testament, 16 times! Each and every time I read it I find a new treasure. A new tidbit. A passion for God's word starts to bubble up in me and I just can't get enough of it. I love it! I am currently at the 17th reading of the entire bible as I am writing this book. My favorite version is the Parallel Study Bible with the NIV and the Message side by side. Reading God's Word on a daily basis keeps me grounded as to my Father God's business. Studying God's Word every day helps me stay focused on doing the things that pleases Him and what an encouragement His Word is! When reading God's Word, select a version that drives you on to keep reading. Some people love the King James, some love the New Living. Whatever you choose, make sure it is exciting enough to keep you coming back for more!

CHAPTER 6

When you combine two of God's most powerful elements, tithing and spending time in God's Word, you are bound to find you are getting blessed in areas you never really thought of as a blessing. One such example is I would go into the Christian book store all the time and look at this beautiful bible that I really wanted. But I would never buy it because it was too expensive for my budget. It was $60.00 and that may not sound like a lot, but when you have nothing, $60.00 might as well be $500,000. (What a change in my lifestyle!) Then one day I went into the Christian bookstore to do my usual browsing and yearning, and this particular day the bible I had so longed to possess as my own was on sale! I'm not talking 10% off. I'm not talking 25% off. It was a whopping 50% off! I was so excited! I bought it on the spot, not even giving my flesh a chance to think about it, reason it out or even be concerned about my financial state. (Note: sometimes we have to invest in our spiritual life, thus making sacrifices in other areas of our lives.) Why I am telling you this is because I love this bible. I want to read it *all the time.* And because of the super discount (my blessing) I was even able to get my name engraved on it! To date I have read 11 different translations, and am planning on reading additional translations. The different aspects and wording from the different translators helps me to understand and live God's Word better.

When you love God and you love His word, you get into the treasure hunting mode that I mentioned above. Although I have read the bible multiple times in multiple versions, there will *never* be a day that I have *read it all and I am done*. God's Word is a lamp unto my feet and a light unto my path as it says in Psalm 119:105.

You have to be so in love with God that you can't wait to spend time with Him. Even if it is the simplest thing as getting a new bible. I look at each and every time I get a new bible and start reading it, as an opportunity to get to know God more. I know all the translations say the same thing, however, it is said *differently* and I look at each of these different translations as a time I am able to find a new hidden gem. Maybe in one of the other versions it was just a dirty little stone, but in this version it may be revealed that it is truly a diamond! I get very excited about reading the bible! Reading the Bible is one of my favorite things to do! If you ask my children, they will tell you that I am a bookworm! A bookworm for Jesus! Many times when they come home from school and I happen to have had one of those coveted days off, I will be sitting on my favorite chaise with my favorite blanket reading God's Word. This is my designated "prayer closet".

I tell my Father God everyday how grateful and thankful I am to Him for letting me stay in this beautiful home and that I will never take it for granted. So many times I have let my mind wander to thinking what I have possibly done to be so deserving of this. And the answer is, has been and will always be NOTHING. I have done absolutely nothing on my own in terms of actions, intelligence or means other than my obedience to what is written in the Word of God. He wrote it, I do it (including tithing) and that is the end of the story. It is because of who God is that He wants me blessed. He wants to give good gifts to me; it's nothing that I can do. But because I want to be pleasing to the Lord and because I want to be obedient to HIS WORD I do and will continue to tithe, because this is what HE expects of me.

- HE rewards those of us who are obedient to His Word.
- HE rewards those of us who take HIS WORD seriously.
- HE rewards those of us who delight in his law and Word (Psalm 1:2).
- HE rewards those who diligently seek him (Hebrews 11:6) and want to spend time with HIM.
- He rewards those who help the downtrodden and the outcast (Luke 14:12-24).
- HE rewards those who help the poor (Proverbs 19:17, 28:27).
- HE rewards those who help the widows (James 1:27)
- HE rewards those who fast and pray (Matthew 6:14-18).
- HE rewards those who stick up for HIM; JESUS, THE HOLY SPIRIT and HIS KINGDOM (Matthew 10:32-33)

God rewards those who tithe. Just like He says in Malachi 3.

CHAPTER 7

I often *review* my journal to remind myself of God's goodness. We are very quick to forget. On one such day I came across a letter that I wrote to our senior pastor, Pastor Robb in 2009:

"I want to thank you from the bottom of my heart for this helpful, wonderful Financial Conference! I feel ignited since I attended this conference. On fire! I lost my job almost one year ago and have been out of work since then. It's been too long. It's been too hard. I was waiting to get that job at the German Consulate which was to start this past December, but did not get it. I need to get a job or start a new career soon. The Strategies for Securing Employment class was very helpful today. I will use some of the things I learned to help me get a job. Friday night was amazing, your preaching was awesome! The third point that you made, "poverty is the result of displaying pride during the movements of prosperity" is what happened to me." I lost everything because I was not living for the Lord and I was not tithing. I am not trying to use that as an excuse, but I was not born again at that time. But thanks be to GOD I have learned since then. I would never think now, not to tithe. Plus I love GOD too much! I once told my former pastor that one day I would like to write a book entitled "From Riches to Rags, (since that is what happened to me) and my pastor replied, "No you should entitle the book as "From Riches to Rags, to Riches!" I thought that was so amazing that my pastor said that and it has stuck with me to this day. I have not started writing the book yet since I am waiting to see what happens next and am waiting on the LORD."

"I want to thank my former pastor who gave me my title for this book." That is what I wrote in my journal in 2009. And to think it was given to me years ago. Wow! When I first came up with the title I thought I was supposed to be waiting for materialistic riches. How wrong I was. I wasn't reading or following the right map. I was looking for a treasure that didn't exist, instead of realizing that I have had riches all along. I am endowed with riches in my walk with My Lord! Praise God!

Do not under estimate the power of the works you do for the Lord. The enemy has done everything in his power to keep me from writing this book. He has put very tragic situations and many distractions in my way. There was a time I couldn't work on this book for a whole month! My intentions were there, but so was the enemy with his creative and crafty mischief. There was one whole month that held one distraction or problem after the next. It seemed they would never stop coming! Just when I thought I would get a breather and finally be able to work on this book, *bang!* The enemy did not want me to pass this information on to my fellow believers because tithing is such a powerful thing *and the enemy knows it*!

One such distraction, which to this day still blows my mind, was a talk I had with my kids about tithing and how important it was. Two of my kids had jobs and I wanted to make sure they were both tithing. One of them was really giving me a hard time about it. (Imagine that! How crafty the enemy is to use those closest to us.) As a matter of fact, and much to my surprise, one of my kids stopped tithing! I flipped my wig! Here I was, writing a book on tithing and my own daughter had stopped doing what I was teaching! I had to get her back on track, and not for the book's sake! For her own well being! She had *willingly and purposefully* decided not to tithe which was so heartbreaking for me. But I did not allow her to excuse her behavior. I continued to talk to her about how important tithing was, and to this day I continue to pray for her that she would see the importance regarding tithing. I want her to be in love with the Lord the way I am! I talk to her almost every day about this but she doesn't want to talk about tithing and always changes the subject when I do want to talk about it! My daughter has the knowledge—she just needs to line up her heart and actions.

Another distraction was one of my other kids was hanging out with the wrong crowd and found herself in a very serious situation that had to be dealt with. And here's a news flash! All of these distractions happened on a Saturday and Sunday. The Sabbath. I found that interesting. The devil never misses a beat. Here I wanted to spend some quality time with our Lord on the Sabbath, and all of these problems/distractions were pulling my time away from the Lord.

Remember this all occurred in a 30 day period! As if that weren't enough, yet another major distraction came to be when some pre-teens decided to vandalize the exterior of my house because they were mad about something that my son had said! However it never the less required my undivided attention, thus keeping me from doing that which the Lord wanted me to do. Write this book. Other attempts to keep me from writing included the teepeeing of my house with toilet paper, nasty, disrespectful writings on my driveway, the egging of my house along with other criminal and despicable activities. And of course, that took yet a whole other Sunday in having to deal with the police and the people who did this!

To say the devil was kicking me when I was down would be quite the under statement, because just when I thought nothing else could possibly go wrong and maybe I had made it through, my house got robbed! My house had never been robbed! I have never been a burglary victim. It was a horrible invasive experience! I would not wish this upon my enemy. And sure enough this happened on a Sunday evening while I was at work. I came home Sunday night, quite tired after a double shift, only to find my house robbed! That took up the whole evening. The police were at my house until midnight trying to figure out what happened. My house was so cold from the officers coming in and out of the house that it was hard for me to keep warm, and my nerves were wrecked. The thieves stole our televisions, the safe, my jewelry, my kid's game systems and games, my daughter's diamond necklace, and a bunch of other items. Those thieves were "want to be" gang members. I needed to remember that the enemy, the real enemy comes to kill, steal and destroy (John 10:10) and he'll use whatever means necessary.

But God in His *awesomeness* turned that robbery around for His Glory. God blessed me throughout this horrible time. The police found the crooks and convicted them for their crimes. Praise God! God turned this around for His Glory in that the police found many of my items that were stolen. They found my jewelry, the game systems and other miscellaneous items. Praise God! As awful as this was, and how justified I *could* have found myself, during this whole time I *continued to tithe.* Believe it or not, this actually drove me to tithe. As a result of my faithfulness to God's Word which instructed me to tithe, *with no asterisks that gave exceptions,* all of these problems were turned around for me *as good* because God is not a man that he would lie as it says in Numbers 23. He promises good to His tithers!

While the enemy was trying to bring me down and keep me down, God reached down every time and picked me up because HE is so faithful and HE always keeps HIS Word. Through all of this I kept praising our Lord and kept spending time with Him in prayer, in worship and in His Word. What can man do to me? Nothing! Psalm 56:1-4 speaks to my innermost being, "Take my side, God—I'm getting kicked around, stomped on every day. Not a day goes by but somebody beats me up; they make it their duty to beat me up. When I get really afraid I come to you in trust. I'm proud to praise God; fearless now, I trust in God. What can mere mortals do?"

To top everything off, I was forced to quit my job right before Christmas! I was a manager at a women's clothing store. I asked my District Manager for a few days off so I could spend Christmas with my family and she said no. She told me that managers could not take any time off at Christmas. I told her that my brother planned a special Christmas for my family, because we have not spent Christmas together as a family (immediate family) in over twenty years and he was having it at his house in Colorado. He had already bought mine and my kid's flight tickets as a Christmas present! I told my District Manager that my dad just had a stroke and my mom was battling (but she is healed thanks to God!)

pancreatic cancer and it was extremely important for me to be in Colorado for Christmas. After all of my reasoning, she still said no. So I had a choice to make, either spend Christmas alone and keep my job, or go spend Christmas with my family and quit my job. Well that is exactly what I did. I quit my job to spend Christmas with my family. It made me sad that I had to quit. Now I am back to the drawing board searching for a job. I am not worried one bit, I am at peace because I KNOW for a fact that my Father God will get me through this also! Guess what saints, since writing this, God did open the door for me with a new job that I really enjoy! And it is because I am a faithful tither! Nothing is too big or too hard for our God! In Genesis 18:13-14 it says, God said to Abraham, "Why did Sarah laugh saying, 'Me? Have a baby? An old woman like me?' Is anything too hard for God? I'll be back about this time next year and Sarah will have a baby." I know He has an over the top, mind-blowing job or career waiting for me. It is just a matter of time. Being a faithful tither has these benefits for me *and* for you:

- Guarantees a blessed life
- Qualifies winning in this life
- Guarantees we are the head not the tail (Deuteronomy 28:13)

Is this good news or what? What amazes me is people try to complicate the tithe by their own reasoning. This is wrong on every level! Tithing is not a complicated command. It is very easy to understand! God told us to give Him 10% of everything off the top. That is it! That is not complicated at all to understand. So please everyone who is reading this book, I urge you to *get with the program* before it is too late! When we are privileged to see our awesome Creator face to face, what excuse will you give Him for not being a tither? Please give this some serious thought. What is your excuse why you have decided NOT to tithe? Who are you listening to? Who will you continue to listen to? The enemy, your checkbook, your bills, your family's desires, or our Father God? Life here on earth is temporary and just a short time. (1 Peter 2:11-12) Eternity is not. It is permanent!

CHAPTER 8

In the beginning of this book, remember when I was spending all that money? Let me tell you about the result of my NOT tithing. Since I was not a tither or living for the Lord back then I lost almost all of "my possessions" which was very, very painful to go through and very embarrassing for myself and for my family. One of the first things that happened as a result of our not tithing was my husband lost his business. He was a very successful business man with a very successful company. He owned his own computer consulting business. He was very good at it and made a lot of money. The company was doing so well that when I first met him, he asked me if I wanted to work for him and be his marketing representative because he needed some help. I had a very good paying job at that time working for a customs house broker, in the International Freight Forwarding field, but I decided to quit that job and go to work for my future husband. I loved working for him and with him. It was very convenient for me since I could work from home and set up appointments as I pleased. He paid me very well for my work.

Even after we got married I continued to work for him trying to bring in more business. We provided computer consulting to all types of businesses. Our consultants were very skilled. They worked on 'mainframes and the old dinosaurs" up to the most modern computer systems and applications. We were making up to $600.00 an hour with some of our clients. It was really great making this kind of money. As I stated earlier, I spent the money so fast my husband could barely keep track, but he did!

To my surprise one day my husband pulled me to the side and told me that he was going to take away my American Express credit card because I spent too much money. As most American Express cards do, this one happened to have no limit on it, so you can imagine the money I spent using it. Looking back on this I feel sorry for my husband who was trying to keep up with the bills I was creating for him. He was a very hard worker and was always such a good provider financially for myself and our three children.

After being married for a short time, one day my husband and I sat down for *a talk*. He told me that he wanted me to be an at home mom. I would stay home to take care of our children and I didn't need to work, but if I wanted to still help him with his business that would be fine. I was okay with that because I wanted the same thing as he did. I wanted to be at home raising our children because they were one of the most important things to me. So I quit working and just concentrated on being the stay at home mom for our children. When my oldest daughter was just a baby I did go back to work at one point working at Arthur Murray's as a professional dance instructor, re-establishing one of my previous professions.

My husband and I lost our company. This came as a total surprise to both of us. One day my husband got a phone call that one of our clients was going to let our consultants go due to the decision to downsize their company. And that is exactly what they did. They fired all of our consultants. In the course of a very short time every one of our clients we had, did the very exact same thing, and fired our consultants. Well as you can imagine with the loss of all of our clients, it's pretty hard to run a company with no clients and so eventually our company went under.

After losing our company, my husband spent years trying to re-establish our company but it never bounced back. And do you know why this happened? We were not *consistently* tithing. We just tithed . . . whenever. I believe this also happened because we were not going to church like we should have. As believers you cannot expect to not follow the Word of God, yet have full rights to receive all the blessings. It doesn't work that way. As I stated earlier, we were skipping church on Sunday in the summer because we were on our boat. Come on! God would surely understand that! It's summer! *"God we love being on the boat! You get nine out of the twelve months! Isn't that enough?"* Are you starting to see the picture here of where our hearts and affections were?

So much of what happened back then is a blur because I have tried to suppress it in my memory. After losing our company I was also concerned about losing our cars since it was very difficult to pay for them without our expected incomes. We had some very beautiful cars back then. Most of the cars we would lease and then trade out every year for a new one. One year my husband ordered a custom made Corvette for us!

What ended up happening was our lifestyle that was so familiar to us, began to disappear, one area at a time. The cars were next on the hit list. We could not afford both vehicles any longer so my husband gave up his Cadillac. We were down to one car, which we were not used to. This caused us to have to engage in the car shuffle that no family likes, but some have to work with because of their circumstances. That's where we found ourselves. So first we lost the business and then the car. Many would say at this point we had been living beyond our means. We weren't. We had money to pay for everything we owned. Remember, the money evaporated.

Next were our motorcycles. No money. No fun motorcycles. My husband was having a spectacular custom motorcycle built for himself. He had to make a decision on what he was going to do about the order as he could no longer pay for it. He put his dream bike on hold. As far as I know he never got it. I remember he bought special helmets for us which were the same color as this motorcycle that was being built. But the dream evaporated, along with our income.

Let's look at this disaster list again. First we lose our company. Then we lose one of our cars. Then the motorcycles. But we weren't done involuntarily downsizing. Guess what was next? Our boat. Our home away from home. We were boat people. We had owned four boats in the past. The last boat we had was a beautiful 45 foot Sea Ray. It was our dream boat! We had all of the trimmings on our boat that anyone could want or imagine. We had Sea Ray embroidered in our favorite colors on the spectacular white leather furniture we furnished the cabin with and on the seats that were outside of the cabin. We even had this awesome design painted in our favorite colors on our other boat which was our expensive Fountain speed boat. We took care of that boat very well and really enjoyed spending time on it. *Even during God's time.* Our three kids grew up on it. *Even during God's time.* I have some of my best memories of that boat. But the problem was it was taking precedent over the time that we should have been giving God. But we wanted a boat, we got the boat, we had the boat and you guessed it! We no longer could afford our beautiful boat, so they took it away from us.

Do you see a pattern here? We very quickly lost everything we owned. And why? Because we were not faithful and obedient to God in our tithing and with our time spent with HIM. I could no longer go on shopping sprees. Remember how much I loved to shop? I was devastated! In fact I had to get a job to start making some money. I started teaching dancing once again at Arthur Murray's. However, that was part time. It was nothing in comparison with what we had been previously making. I started teaching German again after I stopped working at the dance studio whenever I had time and that was not very much money either. At one point I decided to become a certified Bradley birthing teacher to make some money.

My husband and I had taken the Bradley classes while I was pregnant with our first child and I really liked this method. This method is known as "husband coached natural child birth". This means that women are able to give birth, drug free. I ended up having all three of our children with the help of this method, at home, with the help of a midwife. It took awhile and hard work for me to become certified, but I did it. I started teaching classes at my home, which was very convenient because I could still be at home with my children. I was able to watch them and take care of them while my husband was not home. But the money was just not enough to pay our bills.

The whole time this was going on my husband was trying very hard to rebuild our company but to no avail. It was sad. Looking back I keep thinking how stupid we were that we had been robbing from God! Had we been faithful tithers these things never would have happened to us. God would have looked out for us. He would have provided for us. Through this very difficult time my husband became very, very depressed. But he would not give up. Still with all of his diligence in trying to make it work, *nothing* came forth from his efforts. The big time money we were used to, we had expected, had banked on, had depended on and had *idolized,* was gone!

Because I was so desperate to try and return to the "*my* land of milk and honey" I changed direction and started to concentrate on my freelance German-English translating business to try to make some money. My mother was German born and raised in Germany, (which I told you about in a previous chapter) and taught me the German language at the same time as she taught me English. So I have been bi-lingual all of my life. When I speak German, I speak it as a native, which means I do not have to translate in my mind before speaking. When I was in my twenties, while I was single, I started *freelance translating*. I have used this gift that God gave me throughout my life. While in and out of jobs, I could always fall back on my translating skills if need be to bring in additional money. Anything to try to put food on the table. I had some business cards made and started getting some translating jobs which was really good, but the money was never enough on my small salaries. I was doing everything in my power to try to make money to put food on the table. To re-cap I worked at Arthur Murray's, taught German *and* I translated when I could get some work. And then I became a certified Bradley Instructor to make some money. And while working these jobs I still took care of our three children which was a real challenge but always a joy. You moms know what I am talking about when you have a job or jobs and then you still have to take care of your children, it can be very hard at times to try and juggle this.

I so wanted to have my old lifestyle back. But my measly incomes were nothing in comparison to what my husband used to make. But I refused to just sit and *hope* life would get better on its own. No I tried and tried. As a result of the lack of money, which caused many heated arguments, our marriage started falling apart. At one point my husband and I separated and he moved out.

The reality of my situation suddenly hit me like a tidal wave! How could I pay for the house my children and I were living in? In my human brain, I didn't even know how I could continue to pay for the house, but now I know it was only by the grace of God that I was able to continue to live in our beautiful three story big townhouse. This townhouse was so breathtakingly beautiful, it was a dream house! I remember the first time my husband showed it to me (before we bought it). We had walked through the front door which led into a huge foyer, and the view was amazing. When standing at the front door a person could look right through the rooms, right out of the back windows which displayed beautiful big pine trees in the back yard. It was a gated community in Burr Ridge, Illinois. Well friend, you probably know where this is headed. Our beautiful townhouse went into foreclosure, but by the grace of God we were able to sell it while it was in foreclosure and we had to find a new place to live. I thank our Father God every day for my parents because they have helped us out in so many, many ways. It is unbelievable. And it was not only my parents. I am so grateful and thankful to God for my in-laws because they helped my ex-husband and me out financially through the years. Not a lot of people can thank God for their in-laws. But I do.

Let's recap; first we lose our business, our livelihood, our car, our motorcycles, our boat and now our house! Wow, is it really worth robbing from God? The very being that can make *anything* and everything happen for you. Wow! That's something to ponder on. But to answer the question, no it is not worth it. Now pay attention to this readers. This could save you from what I went through. When you choose to steal from God, He *will not* bless you! He can't. He doesn't reward disobedience. You live with the windows of Heaven closed.

Back to the townhouse. We were so close to losing the house I have no idea how we were able to keep it. It went into foreclosure because we could not afford the mortgage any longer and we kept falling behind in our payments. It was by the grace of God that we did not lose it before selling it! We were able to sell it and move on to something else. We lost other items. Men call them *toys* and they are by far too many to mention here. But just use your imagination. Backtracking a little bit, while our townhouse was in foreclosure and when my husband and I first separated, I remember not having any money to buy food for our three kids. My soon to be ex had no job. I had no job. That was so scary to me, I had to take action. Desperate times call for desperate measures. I still had a lot of very expensive jewelry! I ended up going to a jeweler in Burr Ridge and started selling my expensive jewelry to put food on the table. While I was doing this I never gave it a second thought. I never had a thought of sadness or loss because my survival instincts were in full swing. The only thing that mattered to me was to provide for my three children and that I had to feed them no matter what.

I have regretted selling my jewelry through the years but not at that particular time. At that particular time the jewelry did not matter to me. What mattered most was my children's well being. The children had done nothing to deserve this radical lifestyle change. They were the victim's of my decision to not do everything God had required of me. Do you see what happened there readers? We have to realize that our disobedience may have adverse effects on those we love the most. But in all this, even though I was not being an obedient tither and we were losing everything, I believe God was doing something inside of me. God was working on me. In Luke 5:36-39 it says, "No one cuts up a fine silk scarf to patch old work clothes; you want fabrics that match. And you don't put wine in old, cracked bottles; you get strong, clean bottles for your fresh vintage wineskins. And no one after drinking old wine wants the new, for he says, "The old is better."" He was working on my heart. God was giving me a wake up call in which He was telling me that I could change into a better person. I could change into the person He made me, an obedient daughter of God.

The money I got from selling my jewelry came in very handy. I spent it on food and only the bare necessities. I did not receive anything close to the actual value of what it was worth. At one point I sold half of my jewelry estate and I remember my mother telling me not to sell any more of it because I would regret it in the future. My mother was so kind she suggested that if I was going to sell any more of my jewelry, she and my dad would buy it just to keep it in the family. That is my mom; she is a very thoughtful and concerned woman.

CHAPTER 9

To put things into perspective, I spent years buying and acquiring materialistic things and within about six months it was almost all gone. That is something to chew on and swallow, if you can. God said He would open the storehouses and pour out blessings on His children who are obedient . . . He did not promise any of this was for the disobedient. Remember in Malachi 3:10 it says, "Bring your full tithe to the Temple treasury so there will be ample provisions in my Temple. Test me in this and see if I don't open up heaven itself to you and pour out blessings beyond your wildest dreams." Why don't you give it a try saints? Test God in this and see what happens. What do you have to lose? Everything!

In the Bible God emphasizes in Proverbs 13:22 that even the wicked get rich but those riches will ultimately end up in the hands of His children who are obedient. And one of the ways a person *must be* obedient to God is by tithing!

To me tithing is like riding a bike. It comes very naturally. I don't have to put much thought into it, I just do it. Whereas giving an offering is different for me in that I have to think about the amount that I want or need to give. Giving takes a lot of thought, whereas tithing does not. To put it another way tithing to me is like eating. I do it because I like it and need it! This is good!

When I was working those part time jobs I was making very little money compared to what we were used to. I remember talking to one of my friends and she had suggested that I apply for food stamps since our income was so low. My first thought was "Food stamps? That's only for poor people. We are not poor!" In my shock my second thought was probably, "How could I possibly apply for food stamps? That would be way too embarrassing and way beneath me." Looking back on those days, my husband would always do the food shopping since he enjoyed it and he would always shop at the most expensive food stores that were around. Every time he would go food shopping he would spend hundreds of dollars! I never questioned it because he wanted the best for us. And now today I mainly shop at Wal-Mart and Aldi for food since they are the most inexpensive stores to shop for food.

While I was still married, I decided to apply for food stamps as much as I didn't want to, but I did and I was approved right away. I remember the first time I had to drive to our county seat to meet my caseworker. She took me into her office and asked me all of these questions (my husband was with me) that were so personal. That experience was so embarrassing for me. I thought how could this happen to me, a person who used to have more money than I knew what to do with? These days instead of actually getting paper food stamps they provide you with a card that looks like a credit card and that is what you use when you go food shopping. I remember when I first started using this card at the stores. I would try to hide it from other people seeing it because I was so embarrassed! I would swipe it real quick and then put it back into my wallet! But now I have to say that whole experience of being on food stamps was one of the most humbling things I had ever had to do in my life, meaning I would do anything to put food on the table for my three children which clearly required swallowing my pride! It's not that I chose to be on food stamps but that I *needed* to be on them to take care of my kids.

Food these days is so expensive so any help I can get is wonderful. I earned very little money in 2011 while working my part time job. I earned less than $15,000.00 for the year. I have talked to many people who have flat out told me that they would never go on food stamps, how would that look to other people. The way I look at it is being on the food stamp program was between me and God, not between me and man. To be very honest there are some people who I never told (including some family members) I was on food stamps because they would look down on me and ridicule me. And who needs that? It will be interesting to see what happens when these people read this book and find out.

Being a single mom has many, many challenges and one of them is putting food on the table. I remember one person telling me that I should also apply for help in paying my bills. But I never did that. I thought the food was enough help for me. I remember one time when I was at the food stamp office and I was waiting to talk with my caseworker when a man approached me and said to me "I hope you don't mind if I tell you that you look very out of place in here. You look too nicely dressed to be on food stamps". And mind you, I never got "dressed up" to go to the food stamp office, but I did always try to look nice, even wearing jeans or something casual. I am very thankful for such a program the government has put in place for single parents struggling. The food stamps were a blessing because at least there was one area I didn't have to worry about. Had I been tithing all along I never would have had to go on food stamps! Get the picture? God is a giver and He gives good things to his children who tithe! In Matthew 7:9-11 the NIV says, "Which of you, if his son asks for bread, will give him a stone? Or if he asks for a fish, will give him a snake? If you, then, though you are evil, know how to give good gifts to your children, how much more will your Father in heaven give good gifts to those who ask him!" If you are not a tither, can I ask you what are you waiting for?

CHAPTER 10

I want to tell you about my most awesome miracle from our Father God. As I told you earlier on I am out of work and am looking for work while writing this book. (Since the writing of this book God opened up a door and blessed me with a new job which I really enjoy!) Also as I stated in my last chapter I earned less than $15,000.00 in the year of 2011. That is not much money for a family of four to live off of! Well I waited and waited for my tax form to arrive so that I could do my taxes, since this is the money I had to live off of until I got a job. I even had to call my former employer seeking my W2 form. Finally it came and I was able to do my taxes and much to my surprise, my friend did them for me for free. I thought I would be getting back what they took out from my paycheck every two weeks, but in fact I got back much, much more money than I thought! This is my miracle from God! And do you know why my fellow saints? It is because I am a faithful "tither"! This is the only reasoning behind it.

Since I tithe, no matter what my circumstances are here in the natural state, God always blesses me! In His word, in Numbers

23:19, He says He is not a man that would lie and He tells us in His word that He will bless His child who tithes! In Malachi 3:8-11 it says, "Begin by being honest. Do honest people rob God? But you rob me day after day. "You ask, 'How have we robbed you?' "The tithe and the offering—that's how! And now you're under a curse—the whole lot of you—because you're robbing me. Bring your full tithe to the Temple treasury so there will be ample provisions in my Temple. Test me in this and see if I don't open up heaven itself to you and pour out blessings beyond your wildest dreams. For my part, I will defend you against marauders, protect your wheat fields and vegetable gardens against plunderers." The Message of God-of-the Angel-Armies." Had I not been tithing and robbing God, do you really think I would be getting extra money back that I wasn't expecting? This is a supernatural thing happening and I thank God every day for loving me so much and for never forsaking me! In Deuteronomy 31:6 the NIV says, "Be strong and courageous. Do not be afraid or terrified because of them, for the Lord your God goes with you; he will never leave you nor forsake you."

Let me reiterate, a very important point here. Had I been tithing all along I never would have lost most all of my materialist possessions back then. Had I been living for the Lord I would have been able to enjoy all of my materialist things with the joy of the Lord. God wants us to enjoy what He so lovingly gives us such as our children, our family, our friends, our home, our jobs, materialistic possessions. He just doesn't want *stuff* taking place of Him.

CHAPTER 11

I have heard people say things like, "I have never tithed in my life. I want to, but I don't know how to go about it." I will tell you how to get started for those of you who are eager. Let me share some words of wisdom before I tell you how. If you have never tithed before but you want to try it, you should. And would you like to know why? Because even if you may doubt, what could you possibly lose, if everything I have told you is true? You have nothing to lose! Or in my case, everything. Only something to gain and that is God's blessings. Okay, so let's get into the *how to* of tithing. The next paycheck you get:

1. Look at the gross amount (before your taxes are taken out)
2. Take 10% of your gross amount
3. Write out a check, take out cash or you can even put your tithe on a credit card
4. Then take your tithe to your local church and drop it in the offering bucket

Can you believe it? It's as easy as that! As I stated earlier, tithing is a very simple and easy thing to do. It is people who try to complicate it because of their self-doubt. God made tithing easy so people would not have any excuse not tithing. A gentleman came up to me one time and told me about his financial problems that he was having. I felt compassion for him at first but when he flat out told me that he chooses not to tithe because he cannot afford it, well that hit a nerve. See saints, this man is outright stealing from God! He justifies his stealing by telling everyone that will listen that his bills have precedence over paying God what is His. Saints you can't look at your bills first and God second because it is wrong. Not tithing goes directly against the Word of God and the Word is God. God is the Author and finisher of all which means everything that you have, God is the provider of your things. So if God is your provider than He must come first. In Hebrews 12:2 the NIV says, "Let us fix our eyes on Jesus, the author and perfecter of our faith, who for the joy set before him endured the cross, scorning its shame, and sat down at the right hand of the throne of God." When God tells you to give Him 10% of your income, then you need to do just what He tells you to, without wavering. James 1:6 in the NIV says, "But when he asks, he must believe and not doubt, because he who doubts is like a wave of the sea, blown and tossed by the wind."

The problem I see with too many people is they want to analyze what God says about the tithe. And then while analyzing, people start making up self proclaimed doctrine. It is crazy to me! First they are going to steal from God and then they are going to make up stuff, which by the way is a lie, and stand on that as doctrine! That my friend is crazy! And do you know why? Because once again tithing is easy, it doesn't take a rocket scientist to figure this out! God wants you to test him. He says so in His word. He says test me and see what I will do for you! In Malachi 3:10 the NIV says, "Bring the whole tithe into the storehouse that there may be food in my house. Test me in this," says the Lord Almighty, "and see if I will not throw open the floodgates of heaven and pour out so much blessing that you will not have room enough for it." Wow! That is so magnificently amazing to me.

Listen to me saints! Why won't you test God in this? This is the only time in the *entire* bible that God says to test Him! So test Him! What do you have to lose? What is holding you back? Don't listen to other people who do not tithe. In Ezekiel 33:8-9 it says, "If I say to the wicked, 'Wicked man, wicked woman, you're on the fast track to death!' and you don't speak up and warn the wicked to change their ways, the wicked will die unwarned in their sins and I'll hold you responsible for their bloodshed. But if you warn the wicked to change their ways and they don't do it, they'll die in their sins well-warned and at least you will have saved your own life." They are the ones who are losing out on blessings instead of listening to the Holy Spirit or even more basic, doing what the Word of God says! Listen to what is right. Listen to what makes sense to God, not to people. I can't tell you how many times I have tried to explain this to people including some of my family members. It is so cut and dry! This is so simple it takes a human to mess it up! There is no grey area to tithing. It's either black or white. You either are a tither or you are not a tither. Are you with me friends? Are you getting this?

CHAPTER 12

Let's go back for a moment as to why I am writing this book. I am writing this book not to make me happy, as a matter of fact it is quite painful having to relive my ignorance, or shall I say stupidity? But I am writing this as a warning to you—other believers! Please take me seriously and listen to what I am writing to you. Don't ever use the excuse, and that is exactly what it is, an excuse by saying you don't have any money to "tithe" because that is exactly what it is. An excuse! You do have the money to tithe because God gave it to you! If you have a job, than you have money to tithe! This is how it works. You get your paycheck and then you tithe off the gross amount. In other words, you get your paycheck and you give God 10% of what you earn on the gross amount—the amount you make *before* they take taxes out. It's as easy as that! I had an intense conversation with my youngest daughter about this very thing. She has been tithing but her last paycheck she did not. I confronted her on it and her response was shocking because she knew better. She told me something I hear so very often from believers, and that is, "I don't have the money to tithe!" Yes, you do have the money to tithe! You do that first before you do anything else. You get that tithe (the money) out of your hands ASAP and that means to your local church! I told my daughters that our local church can automatically withdraw their tithe out of their accounts if they prefer. Hearing this from my daughter was heart wrenching! She knew I was writing this book about tithing and she chose not to. It really made me mad to think she was robbing God. I understand she is still learning and doesn't understand the ramifications of NOT tithing.

Let me tell you how faithful God has been to my mother. She is a walking miracle! My mother has been battling pancreatic cancer and she had the Whipple procedure also known as the Kausch-Whipple procedure done. During this operation she lost a lot of blood and my family didn't think she was going to live. But saints I never gave up hope in God. I knew she was going to pull through and boy did she! God healed her completely of this terrible cancer! Praise God! Right before Christmas in 2011, the doctors were concerned some of the cancer had come back, so they took a bunch of tests. My mom was very concerned. However she has a lot of faith in God and she never lost hope. Not only was she praying for herself, but I was praying for her along with some other people. After Christmas she got the results back from the tests and guess what saints? She is still cancer free! And do you know why? Because I am a tither. See when a person chooses to be a tither, not only is his or her immediate family protected, but also his or her extended family as well! Are you getting this friends?

Even if certain family members in your family do not tithe (let's say because they do not understand it yet) you can be a blessing to them if you are a tither. Your family can be beneficiaries of your blessing. You may be asking how that is possible. Well I can tell you that it is possible because it happened in my family and I am living proof that this can happen. (Galatians 3:8) Your blessings can overflow to other family members. I can prove this for unsaved family members. If you keep praying for a family member to get saved, there is a lot of hope, right? Well the same thing is true if a family member does not tithe because that person is not saved, so how can they possibly understand? That is why we as tithers can pray for our family members that first and foremost they get saved and second that they would learn and understand what tithing is. See, if a person is not saved then that person thinks that tithing is all about the money going into man's hands, but that is not what it is at all. A person thinks the church *just wants his/her money*. And yes, it does go into a man's hands, but that man is just God's receptacle. This person doesn't understand the concept of tithing and the importance of the tithe to God.

One of these *things* is being obedient to God and what He says. But with a fellow believer who understands why the tithe is important but *chooses* not to tithe because of greed, this person is worse off than the unbeliever who just doesn't know any better. To you fellow believers I challenge you to sit down and write a list of the reasons why you choose not to tithe and then write down the benefits you don't receive from not tithing. Then I would suggest if you are not tithing, do it once and see what happens after that first time, and then sit down and write a list of the benefits that you have experienced from that first tithe! As most of you know Jesus is a Jew and he is very good with money. We have a God who is rich. He doesn't need our money. He just wants to see who really loves Him by being obedient to the tithe. In 1 Timothy 6:17-19 it says, "Tell those rich in this world's wealth to quit being so full of themselves and so obsessed with money, which is here today and gone tomorrow. Tell them to go after God, who piles on all the riches we could ever manage—to do good, to be rich helping others, to be extravagantly generous. If they do that, they'll build a treasury that will last, gaining life that is truly life." In 1 Samuel 15:22 it says obedience is better than sacrifice. I think we should consider heeding this advice.

I am pleading with you to start tithing if you have not yet. Don't question it. Just do it! This is my plea to you. Look at my life testimony what I am writing in this book and then decide whether you will choose to become a tither. Everything I have written in this book is the truth about my life experiences. I ask, if you remember one thing from this book is that you can *choose* to live your life for God and *with* God and become a tither and just watch how much God will bless you, or you can choose not to tithe and there will be no blessing from God.

Saints we are running out of time down here on this earth. Why not turn your life around for God for the good? It is never too late! I have experienced God's riches and goodness in so many ways that I am in complete awe! Not only has our God blessed me financially all of these years, but He has also blessed me in other areas of my life such as my kids and my family. He has also healed me, my children and my family, and it is all because I am a tither!

Looking at my life now compared to how it was when it was all about "my stuff", I see how rewarding my life is as opposed to back then. Today I live my life for and through God, Jesus and His Holy Spirit. In His goodness He always rewards me with good things (experiences) ever day! I'm not talking about every other day saints; I'm talking about every day! I am so tuned into our Lord and what He wants of me, that I see Him doing something loving for and to me every day! This is love because He is love! Our Creator is so awesome! I cannot comprehend why He is so good to me because I am a sinner and I am so unworthy to come before Him. But I know that He delights in me when I am a tither and when I am obedient to Him and His Word. He smiles down at me and hugs me when he sees this in me! His goodness comforts me in this hard and dark world that we live in. I want to cleave and hold fast to Him in every way. I want to be pleasing to Him in all that I do. He is our everything, He is the reason why we are living here on earth, He loves each and every one of us, He takes awesome care of each of us, He sacrificed His only Begotten Son for us (our sins), what can we possibly do for Him? How much do you care about His feelings? Do they matter to you? What matters to you in your life? We are not of this world. We are heaven material. I can tell you one thing saints; this world has nothing for me.

The question I put to you today is what is this world to you? Do you place more importance on the things of this world then on our Father God who art in heaven and His will in your life? Please answer this question honestly. When are you going to start making it about our Father's business and about what He wants and not what you want? This is your chance to prove to our Father that it is all about HIM and HIS Will, and you can start right now by becoming a TITHER!!!